## DATE DUE

| | |
|---|---|
| | |
| | |
| | |
| | |
| | |
| | |
| | |
| | |
| | |
| | |
| | |
| | |
| | |
| | |
| | |
| | |
| | PRINTED IN U.S.A. |

WILDLAND FIREFIGHTER

WILD JOBS

# LAURA K. MURRAY

CREATIVE EDUCATION · CREATIVE PAPERBACKS

**PUBLISHED BY CREATIVE EDUCATION AND CREATIVE PAPERBACKS**
P.O. Box 227, Mankato, Minnesota 56002
Creative Education and Creative Paperbacks are
imprints of The Creative Company
www.thecreativecompany.us

**DESIGN AND PRODUCTION** by Joe Kahnke
Art direction by Rita Marshall
Printed in the United States of America

**PHOTOGRAPHS** by Alamy (13UG 13th, age fotostock, Sergio Azenha,
Burningham News, PJF Military Collection, REUTERS, Michael Routh,
ZUMA Press, Inc.), Getty Images (CORBIS/Historical, Darin Oswald/
Idaho Statesman/MCT, Justin Sullivan), iStockphoto (NeilLockhart),
LostandTaken.com, Shutterstock (WOLF AVNI, BOV, Husjak,
KentaStudio, Martin Klingele, Betti Luna, Nik Merkulov, Miloje, Steve
Photography, USJ)

Library of Congress Cataloging-in-Publication Data
Names: Murray, Laura K., author.
Title: Wildland firefighter / Laura K. Murray.
Series: Wild Jobs.
Includes bibliographical references and index.
Summary: A brief exploration of what wildland firefighters do on the job,
including the equipment they use and the training they need, plus real-life
instances of famous smokejumpers parachuting in to fight fires.
Identifiers: ISBN 978-1-60818-926-7 (hardcover) / ISBN 978-1-62832-
542-3 (pbk) / ISBN 978-1-56660-978-4 (eBook)
This title has been submitted for CIP processing under LCCN 2017940122.

CCSS: RI.1.1, 2, 3, 4, 5, 6, 7; RI.2.1, 2, 4, 5, 6; RI.3.1, 2, 5, 7; RF.1.1, 3, 4; RF.2.3, 4

**FIRST EDITION** HC 9 8 7 6 5 4 3 2 1
**FIRST EDITION** PBK 9 8 7 6 5 4 3 2 1

# CONTENTS

# SMOKE BILLOWS FROM THE TREES.

The fire has formed blazing walls of flames. You feel its scorching heat. Your pack is heavy. But you keep digging your shovel into the soil.

# 1
# WILD WORK

Wildland firefighters control **WILDFIRES**. They try to keep the fires from spreading. They locate and put out **HOT SPOTS**. They spray foam and water. They cut down burning trees.

Handcrews make **FIRELINES**. Some of these highly trained workers are called hotshots. Engine crews drive off-road fire engines.

Smokejumpers parachute into the burning flames. **HELITACK** crews fly helicopters. They may **RAPPEL** to the ground to fight the fires.

# FIGHTING HARD

Wildland firefighting is hard and dangerous work. The firefighters work and sleep outside. They hike, crawl, and dig through rugged wilderness. They can become trapped within the hot, raging flames.

Some firefighters work only during wildfire season. Others work full time. When they are not fighting fires, they take care of trails. They help with **PRESCRIBED BURNS** to keep the forests healthy.

# 3 BECOMING FIREPROOF

Wildland firefighters must be at least 18 years old. They train in the classroom and outdoors. They get a **CERTIFICATION** called a red card.

Firefighters wear a fireproof shirt and pants. They need boots and a hard hat. They carry backpack pumps with water or foam. They have tools like axes or chainsaws. They also carry a small tent called a fire shelter.

# 4
# SMOKEJUMPING BEGINNINGS

Smokejumping began in Idaho in 1940. The parachutes helped firefighters reach fires much faster. In 1981, Deanne Shulman became the first woman smokejumper.

EARLY SMOKEJUMPER

# IS FIREFIGHTING FOR YOU?

Wildland firefighters work to keep people, buildings, and forests safe. Would *you* want to be a wildland firefighter when you grow up?

# YOU BE THE WILDLAND FIREFIGHTER!

Imagine you are a wildland firefighter. Read the questions below about your wild job. Then write your answers on a separate sheet of paper. Draw a picture of yourself as a wildland firefighter!

**My name is _____. I am a wildland firefighter.**

1. What gear do you need for fighting fires?
2. What type of crew are you on?
3. How do you keep the fire from spreading?
4. What sounds do you hear near a wildfire?
5. Why is your job important?

# GLOSSARY

**CERTIFICATION:** proof of certain skills

**FIRELINES:** areas of land that are dug or cleared to stop a fire from spreading

**HELITACK:** a type of firefighting crew that travels by helicopter to fight fires

**HOT SPOTS:** active parts of the fire

**PRESCRIBED BURNS:** planned fires

**RAPPEL:** to move down from a high place using a rope

**WILDFIRES:** fires that occur in the wilderness

# READ MORE

Goldish, Meish. *Smokejumpers.*
New York: Bearport, 2014.

Raum, Elizabeth. *Wildfire!*
North Mankato, Minn.: Amicus, 2017.

# WEBSITES

**Forest Puzzles**
*http://www.omsi.edu/exhibitions/forestpuzzles/*
Learn about the importance of healthy forests.

**Smokey for Kids**
*https://smokeybear.com/en/smokey-for-kids*
Play games and learn how to prevent wildfires.

Note: Every effort has been made to ensure that the websites listed above are suitable for children, that they have educational value, and that they contain no inappropriate material. However, because of the nature of the Internet, it is impossible to guarantee that these sites will remain active indefinitely or that their contents will not be altered.

# INDEX